Lexile: 450L

AR/BL: ______________

AR Points: ____________

DWARF PLANETS

Alexis Roumanis

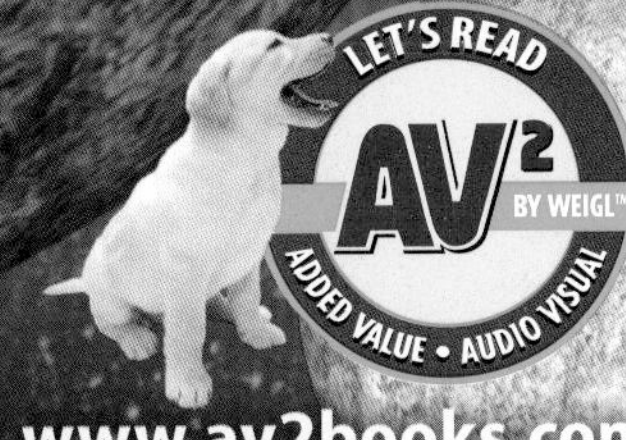

www.av2books.com

Go to www.av2books.com, and enter this book's unique code.

BOOK CODE

P636675

AV² by Weigl brings you media enhanced books that support active learning.

AV² provides enriched content that supplements and complements this book. Weigl's AV² books strive to create inspired learning and engage young minds in a total learning experience.

Your AV² Media Enhanced books come alive with...

Audio
Listen to sections of the book read aloud.

Video
Watch informative video clips.

Embedded Weblinks
Gain additional information for research.

Try This!
Complete activities and hands-on experiments.

Key Words
Study vocabulary, and complete a matching word activity.

Quizzes
Test your knowledge.

Slide Show
View images and captions, and prepare a presentation.

... and much, much more!

Published by AV² by Weigl
350 5th Avenue, 59th Floor New York, NY 10118
Websites: www.av2books.com www.weigl.com

Library of Congress Cataloging-in-Publication Data

Roumanis, Alexis, author.
Dwarf planets / Alexis Roumanis.
pages cm. -- (Planets)
Includes index.
ISBN 978-1-4896-3312-5 (hard cover : alk. paper) -- ISBN 978-1-4896-3313-2 (soft cover : alk. paper) -- ISBN 978-1-4896-3314-9 (single user ebook) -- ISBN 978-1-4896-3315-6 (multi-user ebook)
1. Dwarf planets--Juvenile literature. I. Title.
QB698.R68 2016
523.4--dc22
2014041515

Printed in the United States of America in Brainerd, Minnesota
1 2 3 4 5 6 7 8 9 0 19 18 17 16 15

022015
WEP081214

Project Coordinator: Katie Gillespie Art Director: Terry Paulhus

Weigl acknowledges Getty Images and iStock as the primary image suppliers for this title.

CONTENTS

What Are Dwarf Planets?

Dwarf planets are round objects that move around the Sun. Unlike planets, they share their part of space with other objects.

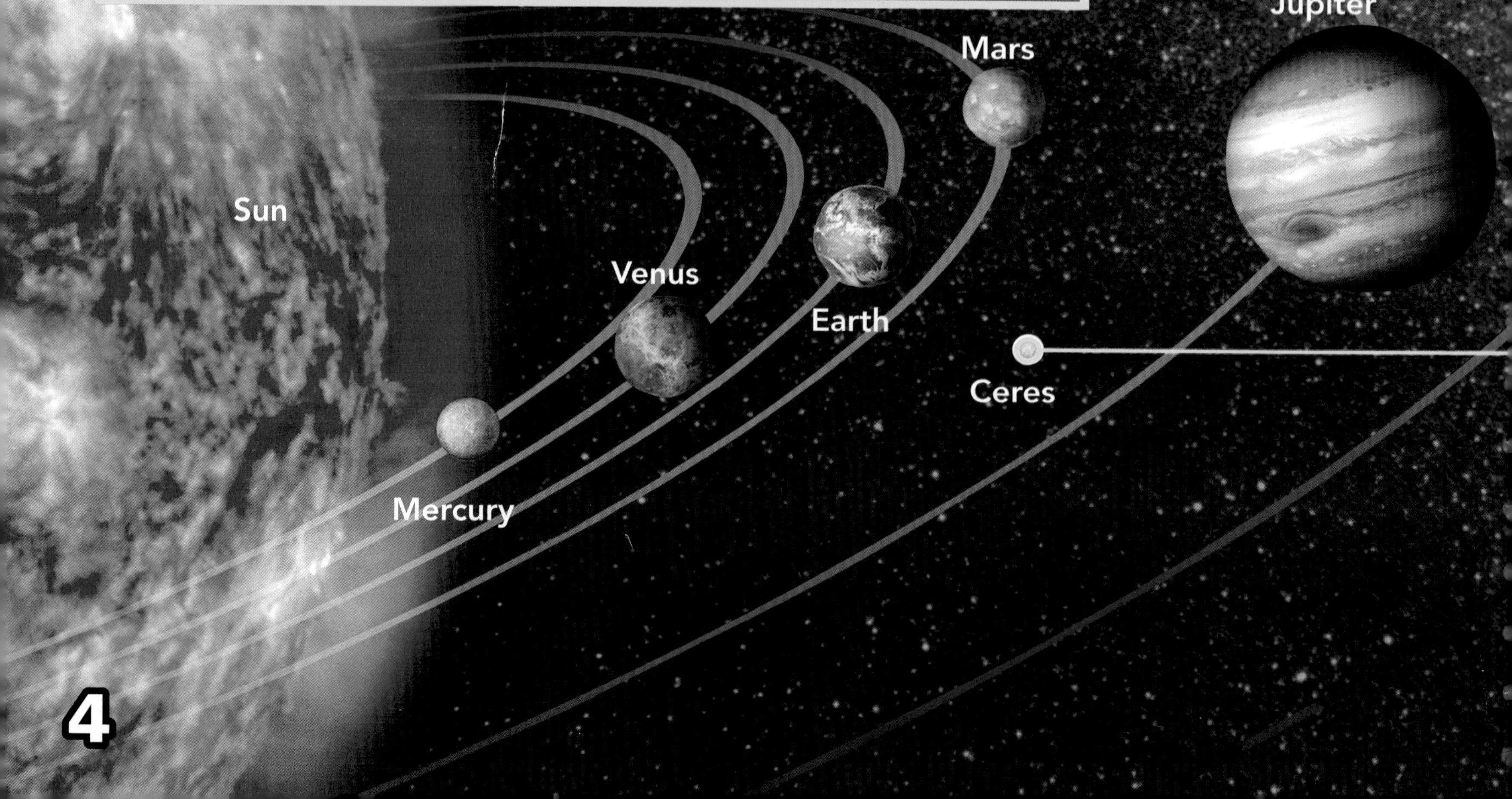

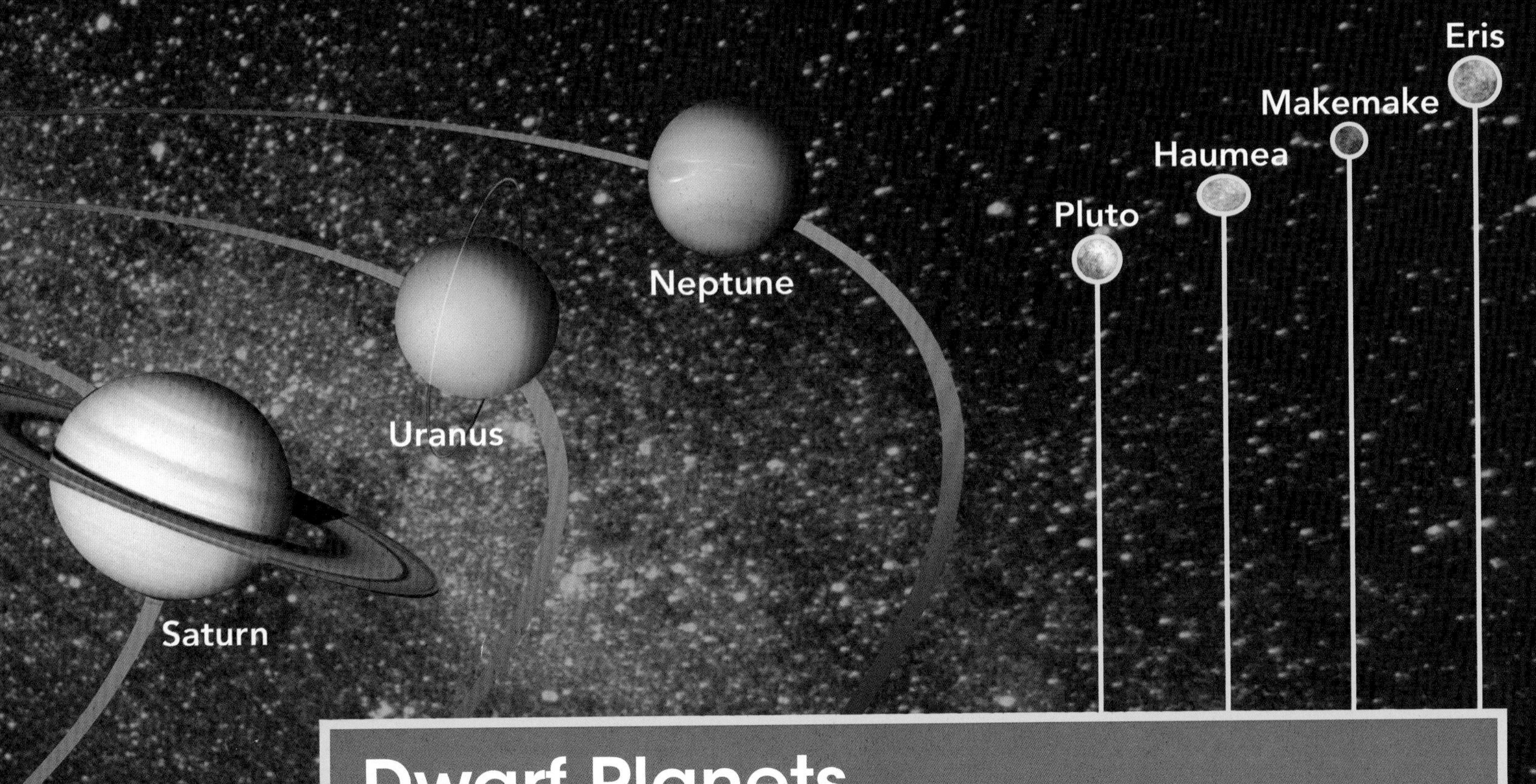

Dwarf Planets

There are five known dwarf planets. They are called Ceres, Pluto, Haumea, Makemake, and Eris.

How Big Are Dwarf Planets?

Pluto and Eris are the largest dwarf planets. They are both about six times smaller than Earth.

Eris
Haumea
Pluto
Makemake
Earth
Ceres

What Are Dwarf Planets Made Of?

Dwarf planets are made of both rock and ice. The inside of Ceres is rocky. The surface of Pluto is covered in ice.

Makemake

Pluto

What Do Dwarf Planets Look Like?

Most dwarf planets are round. The dwarf planet Haumea has a different shape. It looks like an oval.

Haumea

How Are Dwarf Planets Different from Planets?

Planets move around the Sun in a clear path. Dwarf planets move differently. They cross paths with other objects.

Pluto

What Are Dwarf Planet Moons?

There are eight known dwarf planet moons. The largest one is Pluto's moon. It is called Charon.

Who Discovered Dwarf Planets?

Clyde Tombaugh discovered Pluto in 1930. He took photographs of stars and saw Pluto moving across the sky.

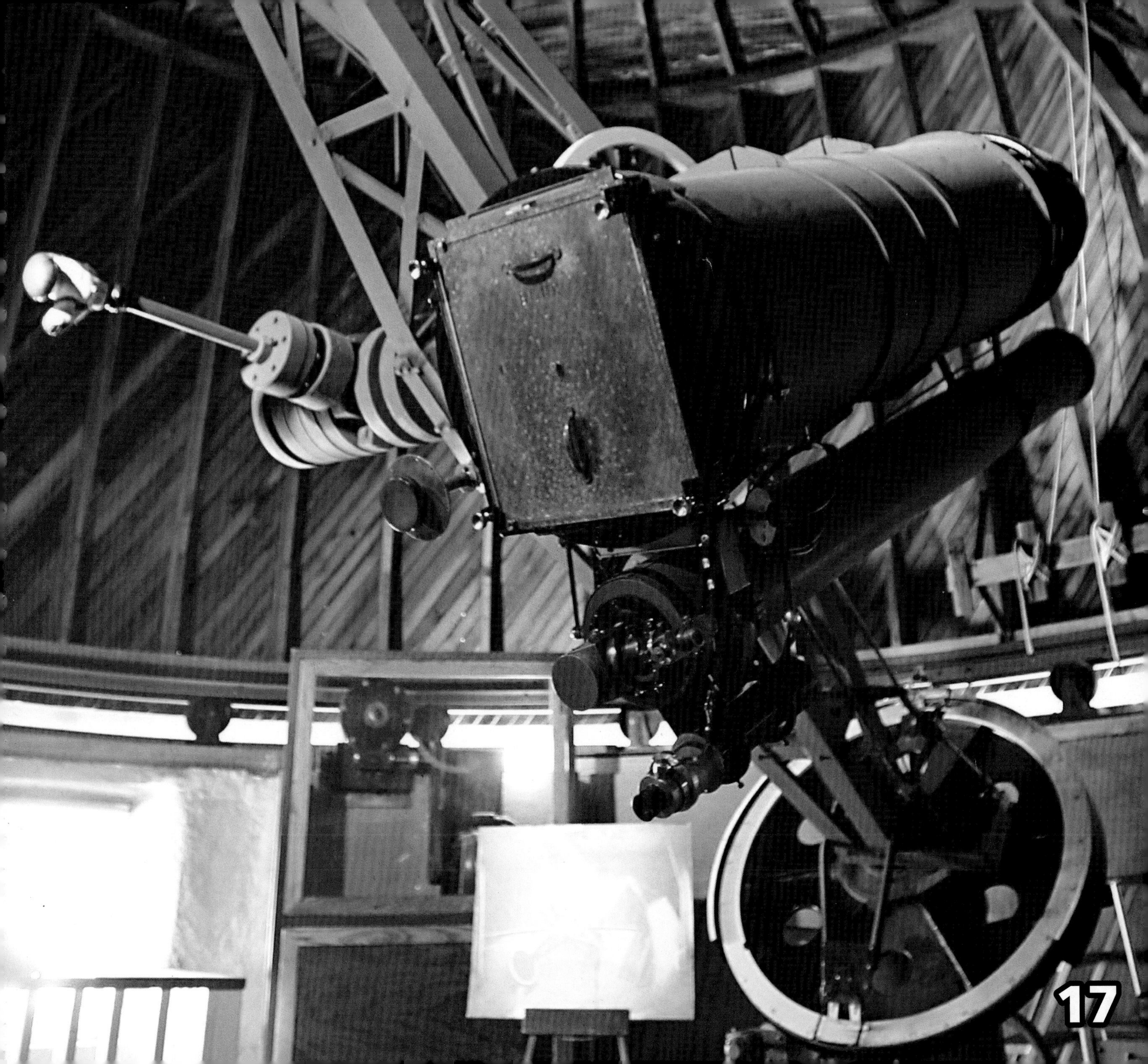

How Are Dwarf Planets Different from Earth?

All planets spin. Pluto spins much more slowly than Earth. Ceres spins much more quickly than Earth.

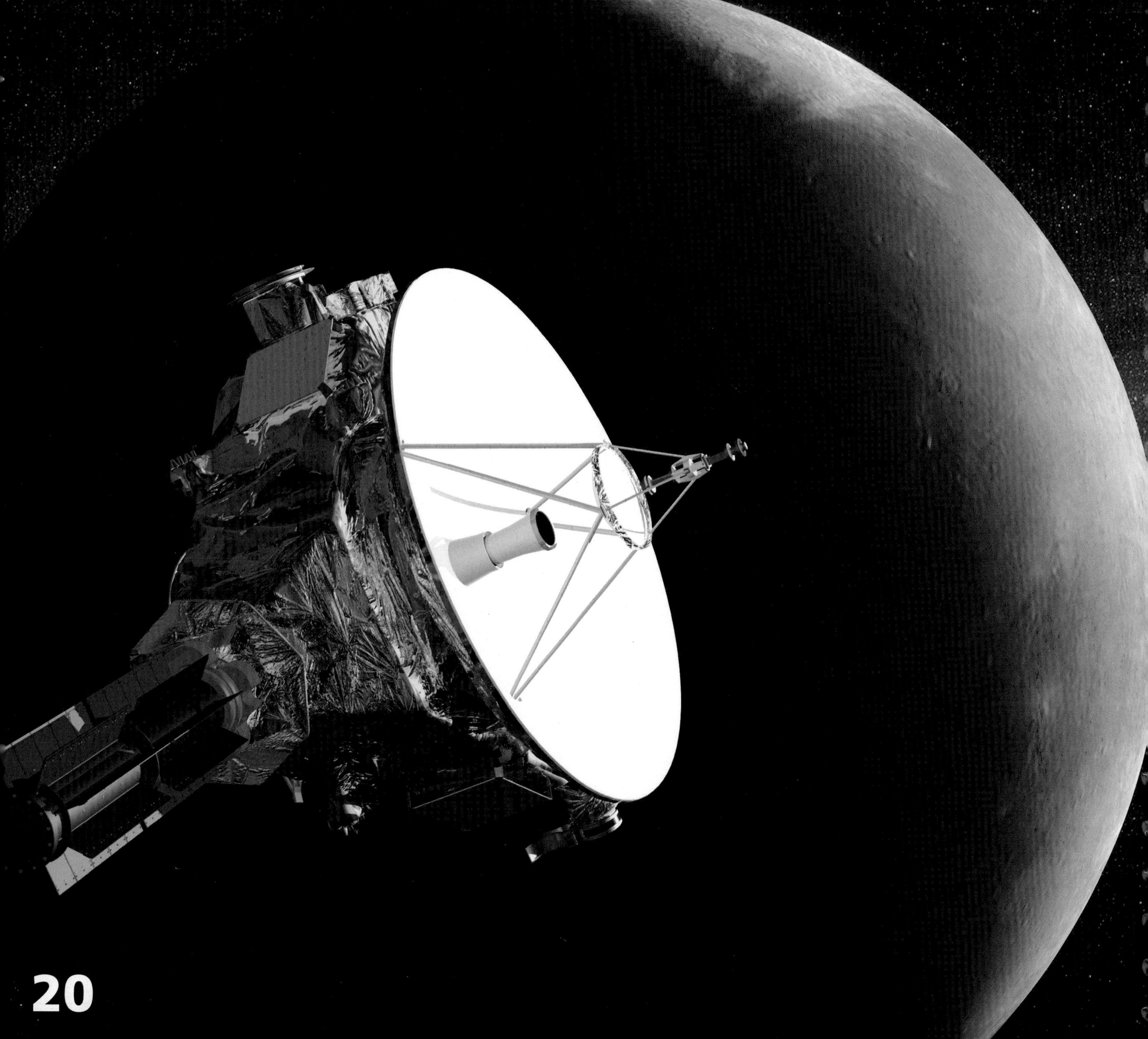

How Do We Learn about Dwarf Planets Today?

Scientists send vehicles called probes into space to study the solar system. Two probes have been sent to dwarf planets. They are studying Ceres and Pluto.

DWARF PLANET FACTS

This page provides more detail about the interesting facts found in the book. They are intended to be used by adults as a learning support to help young readers round out their knowledge of each planet featured in the *Planets* series.

Pages 4–5

Dwarf planets are round objects that move around the Sun. Earth's solar system has eight planets, five known dwarf planets, and many other space objects. Ceres is the closest dwarf planet to the Sun, but it is still 257,055,204 miles (413,690,250 kilometers) away. It takes 4.6 Earth years for Ceres to make one orbit around the Sun. The other four dwarf planets are farther from the Sun than any planet.

Pages 6–7

Pluto and Eris are the largest dwarf planets. Pluto was once classified as a planet. When Eris was discovered in 2005, some experts thought it was bigger than Pluto. In 2006, the International Astronomical Union met to see if Eris should become the tenth planet. Instead, they chose to call Pluto and Eris dwarf planets. Since 2006, astronomers have found that Pluto may be slightly larger than Eris.

Pages 8–9

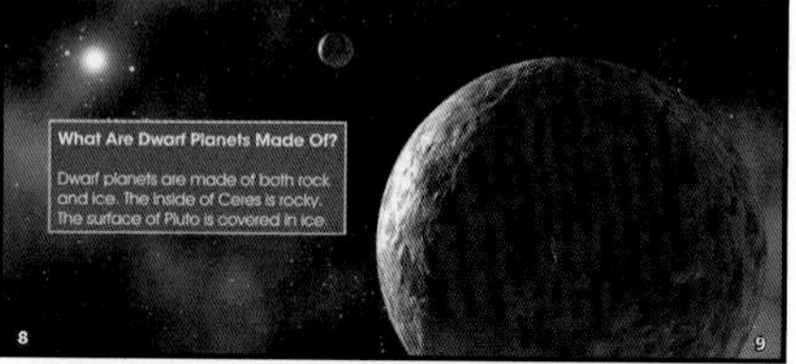

Dwarf planets are made of both rock and ice. There may still be hundreds of dwarf planets to be discovered. They were likely formed when the solar system was young. There is still much to be learned about dwarf planets. They may help scientists understand more about the origins of the solar system.

Pages 10–11

Most dwarf planets are round. Scientists believe that Haumea gets its odd shape because it is one of the fastest spinning large objects in the solar system. One day on Haumea is only four hours long. Dwarf planets can look very different from one another. They can range in color, depending on what they are made of. Pluto looks red, while Ceres looks brown, and Haumea is gray.

Pages 12–13

Planets move around the Sun in a clear path. Like planets, dwarf planets orbit the Sun, and they are rounded in shape. However, unlike a planet, a dwarf planet has not cleared the area around its orbit. This means that a dwarf planet shares its region of space with other objects, such as asteroids. Planets orbit the Sun in a nearly circular shape, while dwarf planets have a more oval-shaped orbit.

Pages 14–15

There are eight known dwarf planet moons. Of the five known dwarf planets, three have moons. Pluto has five moons, Haumea has two moons, and Eris has one moon. Charon is Pluto's largest moon. At almost half Pluto's size, Charon is so large that Pluto and Charon are sometimes called a double dwarf planet system.

Pages 16–17

Clyde Tombaugh discovered Pluto in 1930. Tombaugh was only 24 years old when he discovered Pluto. He worked at the Lowell Observatory in Arizona, where he took photographs of the sky at night. Tombaugh spent hours looking at the photographs and comparing them with one another. In the photographs, he could see Pluto moving, while the stars stayed in the same place.

Pages 18–19

All planets spin. The time it takes for a planet or a dwarf planet to spin once on its axis is the length of a day. This takes 24 hours on Earth. Pluto spins more slowly than Earth, so it has a longer day. On Pluto, a day takes 153 Earth hours. Ceres spins more quickly, so it has a shorter day. On Ceres, a day is only 9 Earth hours long.

Pages 20–21

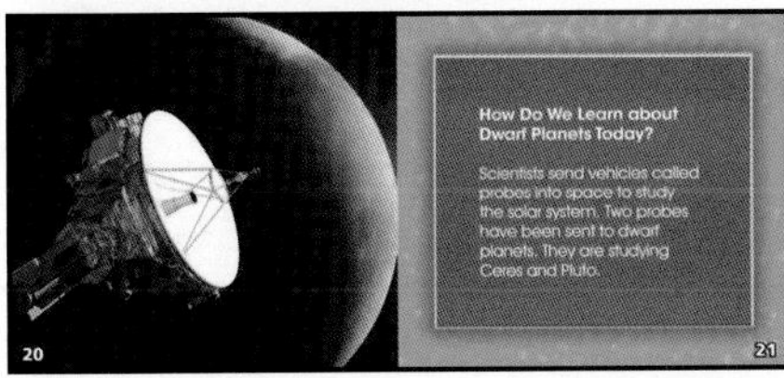

Scientists send vehicles called probes into space to study the solar system. *New Horizons* is the first probe to study Pluto. It will continue past Pluto to study other dwarf planets as well. Its instruments can study the atmospheres, surfaces, and interiors of dwarf planets. In 2011, *Dawn* became the first space probe to orbit an object in the asteroid belt between Mars and Jupiter. *Dawn* is the first space probe to study Ceres.

KEY WORDS

Research has shown that as much as 65 percent of all written material published in English is made up of 300 words. These 300 words cannot be taught using pictures or learned by sounding them out. They must be recognized by sight. This book contains 50 common sight words to help young readers improve their reading fluency and comprehension. This book also teaches young readers several important content words. These words are paired with pictures to aid in learning and improve understanding.

Page	Sight Words First Appearance
4	are, around, move, of, other, part, that, the, their, they, what, with
5	and, there
6	about, big, both, Earth, how, than, times
8	in, is, made
11	a, an, different, do, has, it, like, look, most
12	from
15	one
16	he, saw, took, who
19	all, more, much
21	been, have, into, learn, study, to, two, we

Page	Content Words First Appearance
4	dwarf planets, objects, planets, space, Sun
5	Ceres, Eris, Haumea, Makemake, Pluto
8	ice, rock, surface
11	oval, shape
12	path
15	Charon, moons
16	Clyde Tombaugh, photographs, sky, stars
21	probes, scientists, solar system, vehicles

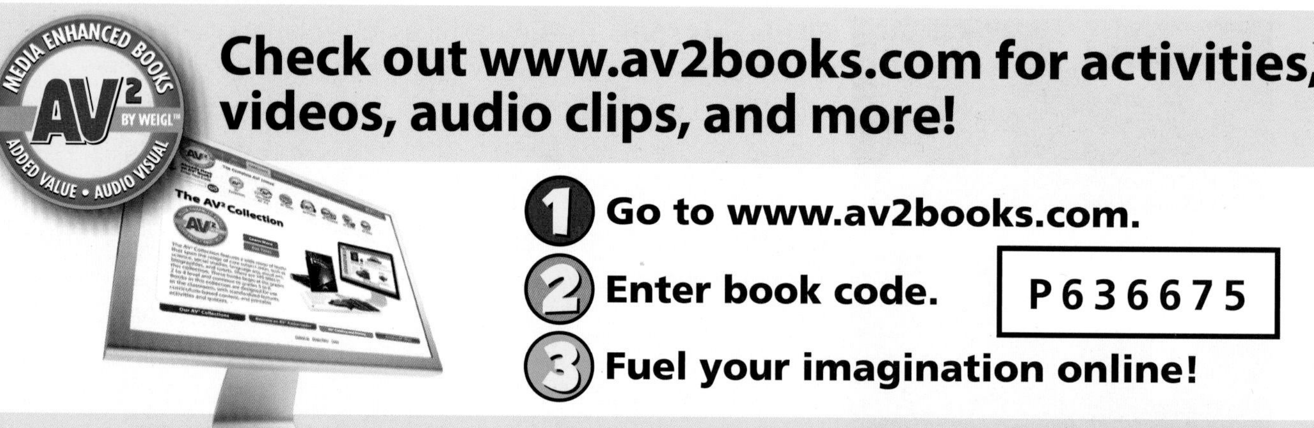